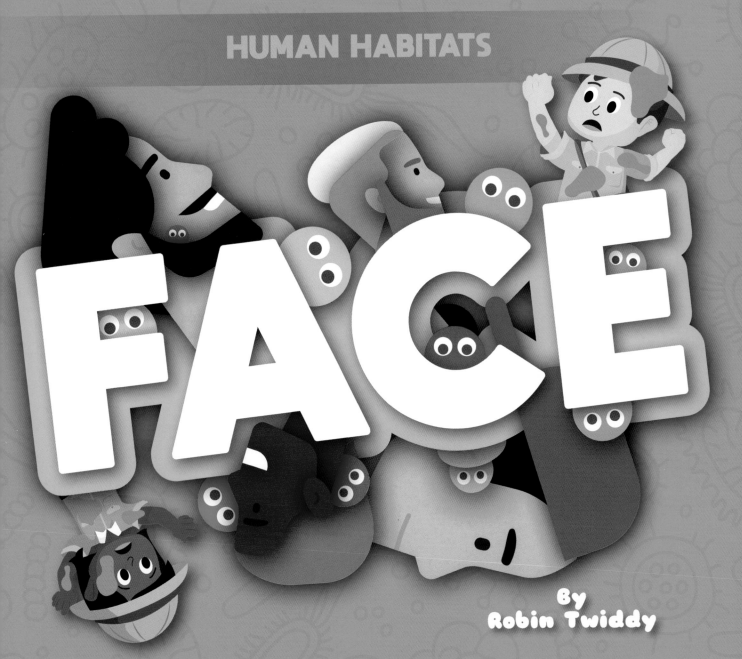

HUMAN HABITATS

FACE

By
Robin Twiddy

Enslow
PUBLISHING

Published in 2022 by Enslow Publishing, LLC
101 W. 23rd Street, Suite 240,
New York, NY 10011

Copyright © 2022 Booklife Publishing
This edition published by arrangement with Booklife Publishing

Cataloging-in-Publication Data

Names: Twiddy, Robin.
Title: Face / Robin Twiddy.
Description: New York : Enslow Publishing, 2022. | Series: Human habitats | Includes glossary and index.
Identifiers: ISBN 9781978523487 (pbk.) | ISBN 9781978523500 (library bound) | ISBN 9781978523494
(6 pack) | ISBN 9781978523517 (ebook)
Subjects: LCSH: Face--Juvenile literature. | Human body--Juvenile literature.
Classification: LCC QM535.T95 2022 | DDC 612--dc23

Designer: Gareth Liddington
Editor: John Wood

Printed in the United States of America

CPSIA compliance information: Batch #CS22ENS: For further information contact Enslow Publishing, New York, New York at
1-800-542-2595

TRICKY WORDS

Bacterium = singular
(one bacterium)
Bacteria = plural (many bacteria)
Bacterial = to do with a bacterium
or many bacteria

Fungus = singular (one fungus)
Fungi = plural (many fungi)
Fungal = to do with a fungus
or many fungi

Photo credits:

Cover - GoodStudio, 4 - Iconic Bestiary, Fun Way Illustration, 8 - SofiaV, 14 - charless, 16 - Pogorelova Olga, Suiraton,
20 - Macrovector, 22 - Julia's Art

Images are courtesy of Shutterstock.com. With thanks to Getty Images, Thinkstock Photo, and iStockphoto.

All facts, statistics, web addresses and URLs in this book were verified as valid and accurate at time of writing.
No responsibility for any changes to external websites or references can be accepted by either the author or publisher.

CONTENTS

Page 4   Welcome to the Human Habitat
Page 6   Features of the Face
Page 8   A Cheek Peek
Page 10   Life on the Lash
Page 12   Guardians of the Eye
Page 14   Surprise Parasite!
Page 16   Hello, Can You 'Ear Me?
Page 18   In the Caverns of the Nose
Page 20   Acne Peaks
Page 22   Squeeze, Pop, Bye!
Page 24   Glossary and Index

Words that look like this can be found in the glossary on page 24.

WELCOME TO THE HUMAN HABITAT

Hi! I'm Mini Ventura. My cameraman, Dave, and I have been shrunk down so we can make a nature <u>documentary</u> all about the tiny things living in and on us. Follow us into the human <u>habitat</u> — a world within a world.

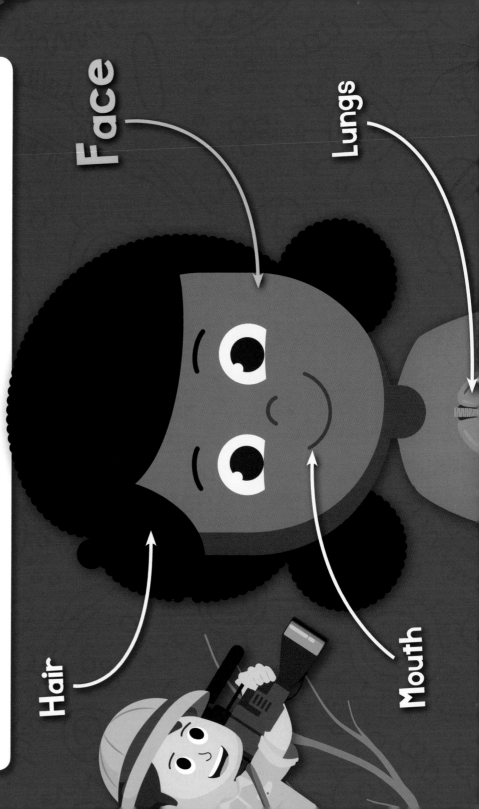

Face

Lungs

Hair

Mouth

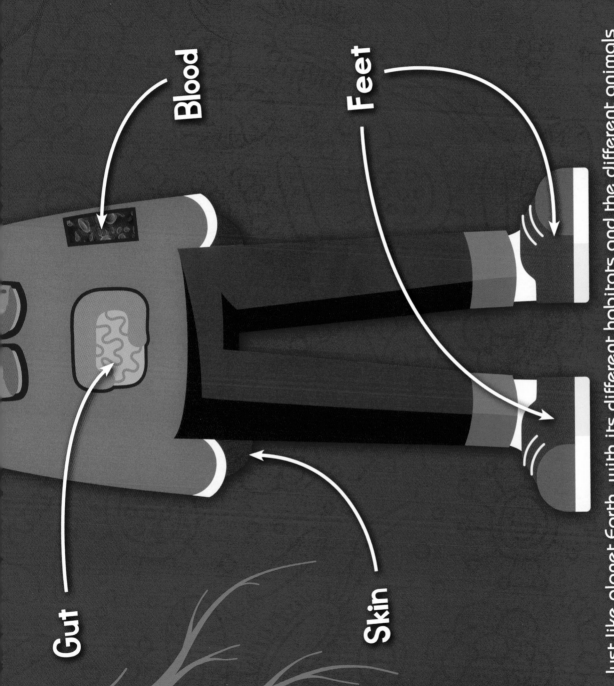

Blood

Feet

Gut

Skin

Just like planet Earth, with its different habitats and the different animals living in them, the human body has many places that are home to lots of tiny living things. Today, we will be exploring the face and just a few of the things living in and on it.

FEATURES OF THE FACE

The human face is a very exciting place to explore. From the open fields of the cheek, to the watery wells of the eyes, the face is home to lots of life.

Nose

A CHEEK PEEK

Can you see all those little holes? They are called pores. Pores let out a special oil that helps keep skin soft and healthy. But wait, I think I see something else in this pore.

These are *Demodex brevis*. Let's call them *D. brevis* for short. They live in pores. *D. brevis* are pretty harmless. In fact, they are quite friendly.

Hang on, I think there is something in ALL the pores!

D. brevis <u>mites</u> are actually related to spiders. Not everyone has them, but most people do.

D. brevis mite

Pore

LIFE ON THE LASH

Wow, look up there – we really are in luck today. There are *Demodex folliculorum* mites climbing up and down those eyelashes. They are a lot like the *D. brevis* mites that we met living in the pores.

I will call them *D. folli* for short.

GUARDIANS OF THE EYE

I have to be careful here. The eye is easily damaged. Oooh, it is squidgy! Can you see the <u>bacteria</u> wandering around on the eye? Believe it or not, they are actually <u>protecting</u> the eye.

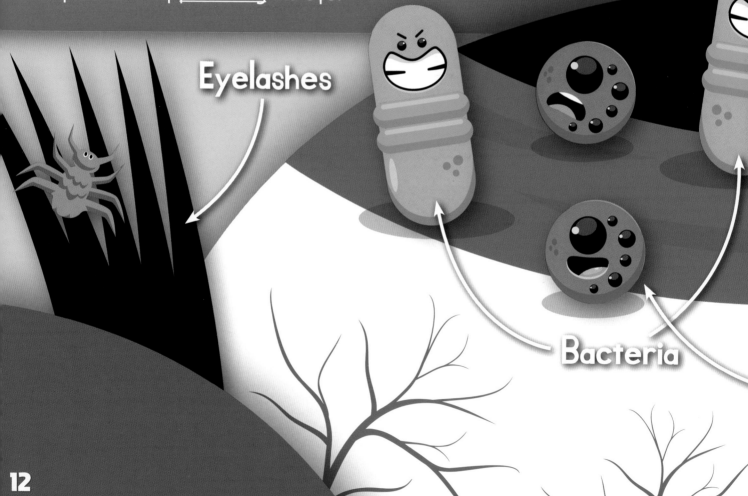

Eyelashes

Bacteria

SURPRISE PARASITE!

There is a *loa loa* worm in this eye. It is very rare to see one of these living in an eye.

HELLO, CAN YOU 'EAR ME?

Well, it was a long long way down here – a long and waxy way down!
Now let's see what we can see in the ear. All that yellow stuff is ear wax.

It's sticky and yucky, but it stops dirt and bacteria from getting inside the ear.

Cockroach

Get out of here, cockroach. This isn't your home!

Look, there are tracks in the wax. It's a cockroach! That isn't supposed to be in here. Sometimes a cockroach will climb into an ear to eat the yellow wax – but it doesn't happen very often.

17

IN THE CAVERNS OF THE NOSE

Here, in the nostril cavern, we find a habitat that is perfect for growing bacteria. It is warm and wet, and a great way for invaders to get inside the body.

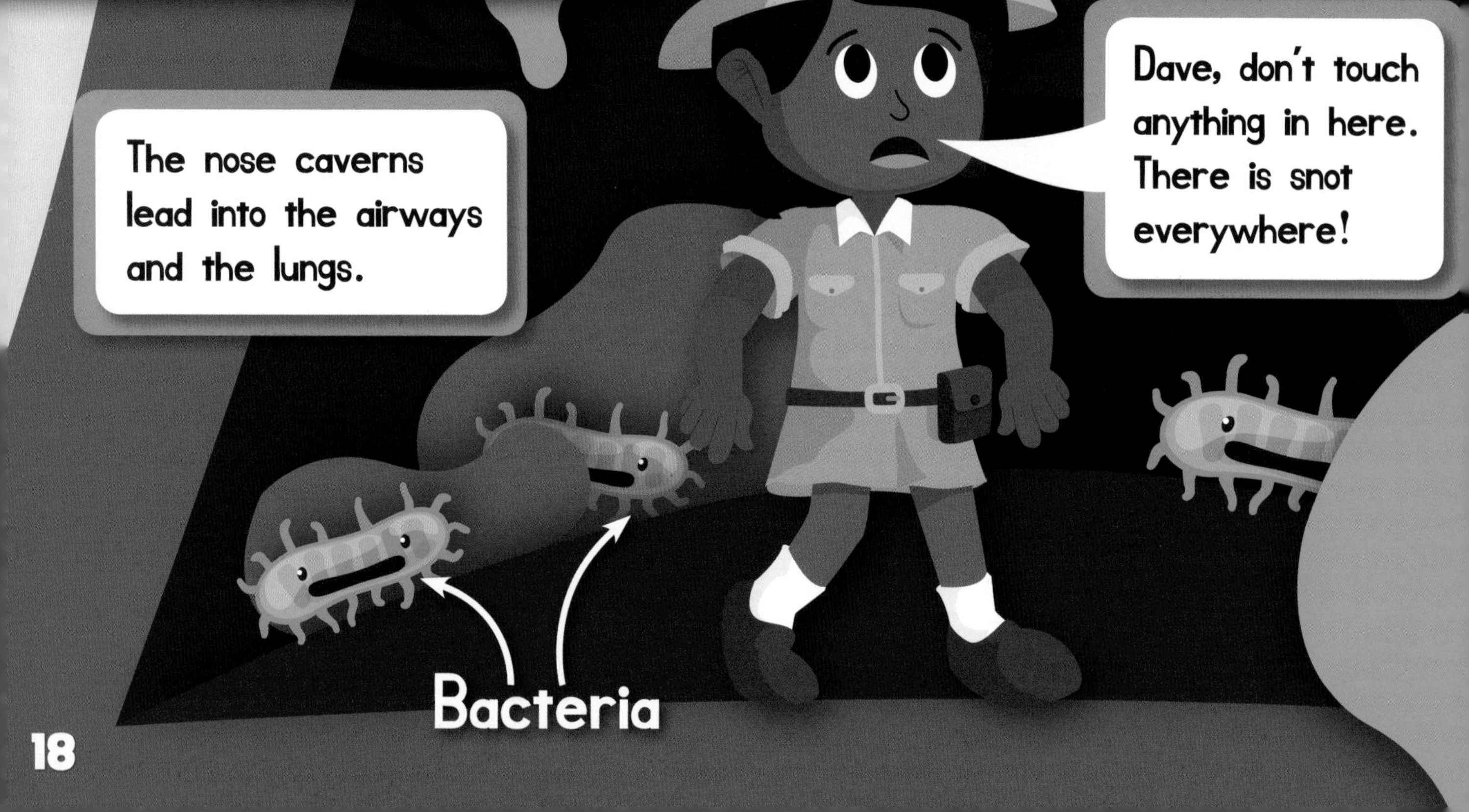

Dripping from the ceiling and oozing down the walls is mucus — but you might call it snot. This stuff has a really important job — catching bacteria, dust, and anything else trying to get into the body.

More snot

Really sticky, gross snot

The human habitat can make up to **1 quart (1 L)** of mucus a day.

ACNE PEAKS

This bacterium is called *P. acnes*. It lives on the skin and can cause pimples just like the one I am climbing on now.

The pimples are caused when bacteria fill up pores in the skin. Do you remember that we saw them earlier? Look at those pores. They will be pimples soon!

Lots of people get acne, and it doesn't matter how clean or dirty the skin is. If there is enough *P. acnes*, then you are probably going to get some pimples.

SQUEEZE, POP, BYE!!

Who knew that there was such life on the human face? From the bacteria making pimples in our pores, to the mites climbing up our eyelashes, there is so much to explore!

GLOSSARY

bacteria	tiny living things, too small to see, that can cause diseases
documentary	a film that looks at real facts and events
fungus	a living thing that often looks like a plant but has no flowers
habitat	the natural home in which animals, plants, and other living things live
invaders	a group of things that have entered a place that they are not from or welcome in
mites	tiny arachnids of the same family as spiders
parasite	a creature that lives on or in another creature
plains	large areas of flat land
protecting	stopping something from coming to harm

INDEX

bacteria 12–13, 16, 18–22
cockroaches 17
eyelashes 10–12, 22
follicles 11
fungi 13

habitats 4–5, 13, 18–19, 23
loa loa worm 14–15
mites 9–11, 22
nostrils 7, 18
oil 8
pimples 20–21

pores 8–10, 22
snot 18–19
spiders 9
wax 16–17